Those Funny Flamingos

Those Funny Flamingos

Jan Lee Wicker

Illustrated by Steve Weaver

Pineapple Press, Inc.
Sarasota, Florida

Inquiries should be addressed to:

Pineapple Press, Inc.
P.O. Box 3889
Sarasota, Florida 34230

www.pineapplepress.com

Library of Congress Cataloging-in-Publication Data

Wicker, Jan Lee, 1953-
Those funny flamingos / by Jan Lee Wicker.
p. cm.
Includes bibliographical references.
ISBN 1-56164-295-9 (paperback : alk. paper)
1. Flamingos--Juvenile literature. I. Title.

QL696.C56W565 2004
598.3'5--dc22
2004005038

Hardcover ISBN-13: 978-1-56164-357-8
Paperback ISBN-13: 978-1-56164-295-3

First Edition
Hb 10 9 8 7 6 5 4 3 2 1
Pb 10 9 8 7 6 5 4

Design by Steve Weaver
Printed in China

For ages 5–9

To my mother and friend, Joyce Lee Riley,
who has shown me the meaning of love

Contents

Why are flamingos pink?

Flamingos are pink because of the food they eat. Has your mother ever told you that you are what you eat? If you eat good, healthy foods, you will be healthy and look healthy. The same thing happens with flamingos. They eat blue-green algae, shrimp, crayfish, and mosquito larvae. These foods have pigments called carotenoids. The more they eat of these foods, the pinker they get.

Why do flamingos have webbed feet?

If you have ever walked in really deep snow or in wet sand, you know that your feet sink. People in parts of the world with lots of snow wear snowshoes (which are like big tennis rackets) so they will not sink. Divers wear foot fins (which look like webbed flamingo feet) so they will not sink in the wet sand and so they can swim. The same is true with flamingos. They have webbed feet

so they will not sink when they walk in the mud and so they can swim in the water.

Why do flamingos stand on one leg?

Think about the reasons you sit or stand the way you do. One reason is because it is more comfortable. The same is true for flamingos. It is comfortable for them to stand on one foot. Have you ever sat with one foot under your leg to keep your foot warm? Flamingos also stand on one foot to stay warm under their feathers.

How can flamingos bend their knees backwards?

The part you see a flamingo bending is really its ankle. A flamingo's knees are close to its body, under the feathers. So flamingos bend their ankles just like we do—forward. Their knees bend backward, like ours.

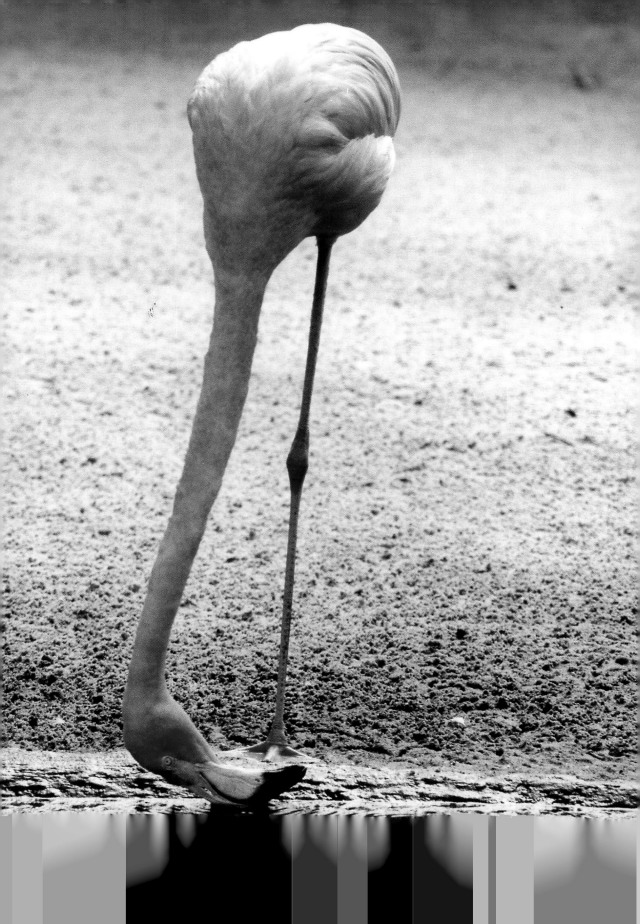

Why do flamingos eat with their head upside down?

Flamingos do this to strain tiny food bits out of the water. Just as humpback whales have baleen to filter their food out from the water, flamingos have tiny teeth on their beaks to do this. By turning their heads upside down and moving their heads back and forth, flamingos filter the food out of the water. The little comb-like teeth keep the food in and let the water go out.

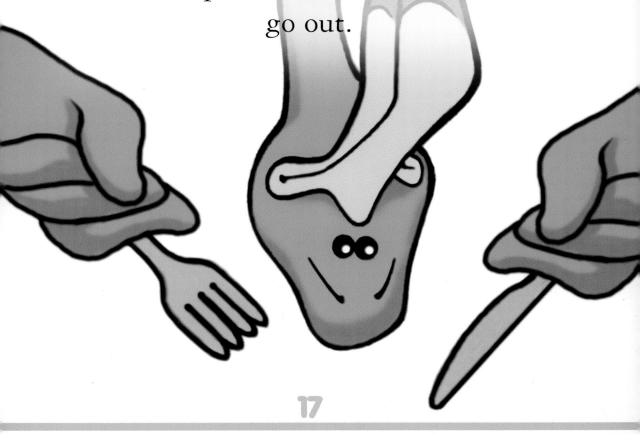

Are all flamingo feathers pink?

No. Although most of the feathers we see are from white to dark pink in color, their wing tips are black. These are the flight feathers. The black pigment in these feathers makes them stronger.

Can flamingos fly?

Yes, they can. You don't see them fly at the zoo because they have their wings clipped. If the wings are pinioned or cut on one side, when they try to fly they can't keep their balance. Because of this, they can't take off. This doesn't hurt the birds, but allows us to see them in open parks and zoos.

How do flamingos stay dry?

Flamingos preen their feathers to keep them waterproof. They do this by using their beaks to spread oil on their feathers. The oil comes from a gland at the base of their feathers.

What kind of nest does a flamingo make?

A flamingo makes a mud nest about 1–2 feet tall. The nest has a dip in the middle for the egg. The nest can weigh from 75 to 180 pounds. Both parents take turns sitting on the egg. The flamingo folds its legs underneath to sit on the nest.

Ostrich

Emu

Flamingo

Goose

Chicken

Robin

How many eggs does a flamingo lay?

A flamingo's normal clutch (how many eggs it lays at one time) is one egg. The egg is usually white, but can be pale blue. It is larger than a chicken egg. It is about 3 inches long. The incubation time (or how long it takes to hatch) is about 28 days. It takes about a day and a half for the baby to hatch out of its shell.

Are baby flamingos pink?

No. They are born without feathers. It takes about 1 month before the babies have feathers. Their feathers are white and gray. They don't get their adult pink feathers until they are 2 years old.

Can baby flamingos stand on one foot?

Yes. It is a comfortable way for them to stand. Baby flamingos also squat on their ankles. Even when very young, they begin to drink with their head upside down. They begin cleaning their feathers as babies also.

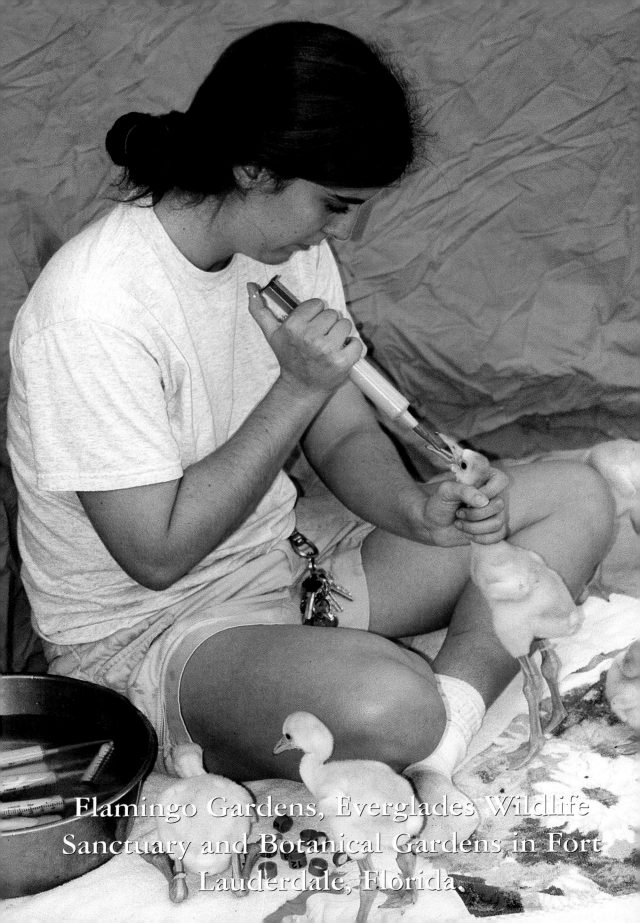

Flamingo Gardens, Everglades Wildlife
Sanctuary and Botanical Gardens in Fort
Lauderdale, Florida.

What do baby flamingos eat?

They eat a liquid diet from the parent's mouth. It is called crop milk. If they are hand raised they eat the liquid from a syringe. Baby flamingos have to be fed every 90 minutes for about 5 minutes each time. As they get older, they feed longer and not as often.

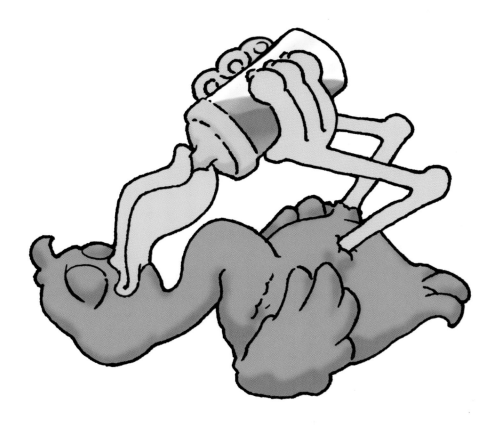

How do flamingos sleep?

Flamingos do not sleep like we do. A flamingo sleeps standing up on one leg. Its head lies on its back, tucked into its feathers.
How would you like to sleep like that?

How big are flamingos?

It varies. The Lesser Flamingo is about 3 feet tall and weighs 2 pounds. The Greater Flamingo can be 6 feet tall and weigh 8 pounds. Flamingos can live to be about 50 years old!

Lesser Flamingo   Andean Flamingo   Caribbean Flamingo

James' Flamingo   Chilean Flamingo   Greater Flamingo

How many flamingos live together?

A group of flamingos is called a flock. In the wild, flocks can get as large as 100,000 individuals! Flamingos feel safe in large flocks, but they will breed (have babies) in a flock as small as 24. Rarely will they breed in flocks less than 24.

Do all flamingos look the same?

No. There are 6 different kinds of flamingos. All of them have black bill tips. They are the Lesser, James', Greater, Caribbean, Chilean, and Andean flamingos.

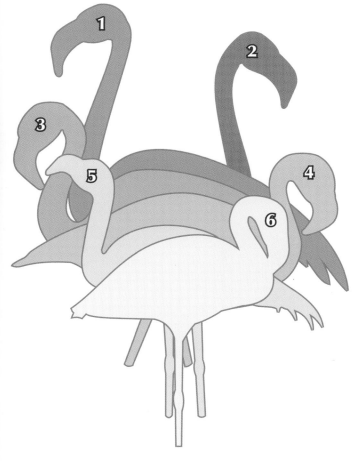

1 Greater Flamingo

2 Caribbean Flamingo

3 Chilean Flamingo

4 Andean Flamingo

5 James' Flamingo

6 Lesser Flamingo

Do flamingos ever lose their feathers?

Yes. This is called molting. Flamingos molt in the late summer. When they molt, they lose a lot of the color in their feathers. Many birds cannot fly during this time. Birds aren't the only animals that molt. Snakes lose their skin. Deer lose their antlers (or horns). Aren't you glad you just buy new clothes as you grow?

Can flamingos salute?

Yes. They salute with their wings by opening and closing them. Males do this to show off to the females, like boys might flex their muscles in front of girls.

Where in the world do wild flamingos live?

Different flamingos live in different parts of the world. The Caribbean Flamingo lives in the islands south of Florida. The Greater Flamingo lives in Africa, Europe, South America and the Middle East. The Chilean flamingo lives in Chile, South America. The Andes Mountains in South America are home to the Andean and James' Flamingos. The Lesser Flamingo lives in Africa.

Greater Flamingo   Caribbean Flamingo   Chilean Flamingo

Andean Flamingo   James' Flamingo   Lesser Flamingo

Activities

1. **Make a flamingo.** You can make a flamingo with your hand and some paint. Paint the palm and fingers of your right hand with pink paint. Press your painted hand onto the paper with fingers closed and fingertips down as shown. Then paint the side of your left hand from the pinky to the bottom of the palm. Press, curved like a C, to add the neck and head. Then paint on the legs with a small brush. Let it all dry. Using a little black paint, add the tip of the bill and the eye. If you have a little yellow paint, you can circle that around the eye dot to make it more real. You could do this with fabric paint to make a flamingo T-shirt!

2. **Make a flock of flamingos.** You can make a flock of flamingos using your thumb, pink paint, a pipe cleaner, a black pen, and a pink pencil. Put some pink paint into a shallow pan. Stick your thumb into it and print a flamingo body as shown. Bend the pipe cleaner into an S shape for the neck. Dip it into the paint and add it to the body. When the paint is dry, use a pink pencil to make the legs. Add a black tip to the end of the bill, then a black dot to make the eye. Make as many flamingos as you want to have in your flock.

Flamingo Cane

Note: This activity requires adult supervision since a hot glue gun is used.

Materials needed: 1 pink pipe cleaner, 1 pink foam sheet, 1 red and white candy cane, black electrical tape, a hot glue gun, 2 pink rollie eyes, 1 pink feather.

Cut the pipe cleaner to 4½ inches. Cut two flamingo feet shapes from the pink foam sheet. Cut off a 1½-inch piece of black tape.

Wrap the black tape on the end of the candy cane and pinch it together. After wrapping the pipe cleaner around the candy cane about 3 inches from the base, bend it to look like a 4. Using a hot glue gun, glue one foot on the bottom of the candy cane and the other one on the end of the bent pipe cleaner.

Glue one eye on each side of the candy cane about an inch from the black tape. Then glue the feather on the back side of the candy cane. Now you have a flamingo cane.

Flamingazine

Materials needed: magazines, scissors, and glue.

Draw an outline of a flamingo on a white piece of paper. (You can use the flamingos shown here as a pattern.) Find items in the magazine that are pink and cut them out for the flamingo's body and legs. Find items that are black and cut them out for the flamingo's beak. Glue them into the outline of the flamingo.

Bits-and-Pieces Flamingo

You can make a Bits-and-Pieces Flamingo the same way you make a Flamingazine. Instead of a magazine, use pink and black paper. Trace the flamingo pattern on a white piece of paper. Tear pink paper for the flamingo's body and legs. Tear black paper for the beak. Glue it on the pattern in the shape of a traced flamingo.

Where to Learn More about Flamingos

Some books about flamingos:

Jacobs, Liza. Flamingos (Wild Wild World). San Diego, California: Blackbirch Press. 2003. (ages 9-12)

Mari, Carol, and Nigel Collar. Pink Flamingos. New York: Abbeville Press, 2000. (photographs of East African pink flamingos)

McMillan, Bruce. Wild Flamingos. Boston, Massachusetts: Houghton Mifflin, 1997. (about the Caribbean flamingos in the West Indies, for ages 9-12)

Pallotta, Jerry. The Bird Alphabet. Watertown, Massachusetts: Charlesbridge Publishing, 1987. (ages 4-8)

Some good flamingo websites:

www.everwonder.com/david/flamingos

www.whozoo.org/Intro98/marisede/marinased.htm

www.nationalgeographic.com/ngm/0312/feature4

About the Author

Jan Lee Wicker has taught children in pre-kindergarten through first grade for the last 23 years. She graduated from Appalachian State University and currently teaches kindergarten in Weldon, North Carolina. Her class mascots, twin flamingo Beanie Babies, were her inspiration to teach her students more about flamingos. She lives in Roanoke Rapids with her husband and has two grown sons.

Here are the other books in this series. For a complete catalog, visit our website at www.pineapplepress.com. Or write to Pineapple Press, P.O. Box 3889, Sarasota, Florida 34230-3889, or call (800) 746-3275.

Those Amazing Alligators by Kathy Feeney. Illustrated by Steve Weaver, photographs by David M. Dennis. Discover the differences between alligators and crocodiles; learn what alligators eat, how they communicate, and much more. Ages 5–9.

Those Beautiful Butterflies by Sarah Cussen. Illustrated by Steve Weaver. This book answers 20 questions about butterflies—their behavior, why they look the way they do, how they communicate, and much more. Ages 5–9.

Those Colossal Cats by Marta Magellan. Illustrations by Steve Weaver. Features lions, tigers, panthers, cougars. Answers 20 questions about big cats, such as why they lick their fur, which cat is the fastest, and why tigers have stripes while leopards have spots. Ages 5–9.

Those Delightful Dolphins by Jan Lee Wicker. Illustrations by Steve Weaver. Learn the difference between a dolphin and a porpoise, find out how dolphins breathe and what they eat, and learn how smart they are and what they can do. Ages 5–9.

Those Excellent Eagles by Jan Lee Wicker. Illustrated by Steve Weaver, photographs by H. G. Moore III. Learn all about those excellent eagles—what they eat, how fast they fly, why the American bald eagle is our nation's national bird. Ages 5–9.

Those Lively Lizards by Marta Magellan. Illustrated by Steve Weaver, photographs by James Gersing. In this book you'll meet lizards that can run on water, some with funny-looking eyes, some that change color, and some that look like little dinosaurs. Ages 5–9.

Those Magical Manatees by Jan Lee Wicker. Illustrated by Steve Weaver. Twenty questions and answers about manatees—you'll find out more about their behavior, why they're endangered, and what you can do to help. Ages 5–9.

Those Outrageous Owls by Laura Wyatt. Illustrated by Steve Weaver, photographs by H. G. Moore III. Learn what owls eat, how they hunt, and why they look the way they do. You'll find out what an owlet looks like, why horned owls have horns, and much more. Ages 5–9.

Those Peculiar Pelicans by Sarah Cussen. Illustrated by Steve Weaver, photographs by Roger Hammond. Find out how much food those peculiar pelicans can fit in their beaks, how they stay cool, and whether they really steal fish from fishermen. Ages 5–9.

Those Terrific Turtles by Sarah Cussen. Illustrated by Steve Weaver, photographs by David M. Dennis. You'll learn the difference between a turtle and a tortoise, and find out why they have shells. Meet baby turtles and some very, very old ones, and even explore a pond. Ages 5–9.

Those Voracious Vultures by Marta Magellan. Illustrated by Steve Weaver, photographs by James Gersing and Ron Magill. Learn all about vultures—the gross things they do, what they eat, whether a turkey vulture gobbles, and more. Ages 5–9.